A Guide to CHANGE

When Your Family Moves

Written by E.C. Andrews

I0807153

Published in 2026 by
KidHaven Publishing, an Imprint of
Greenhaven Publishing, LLC
2544 Clinton St., Buffalo, NY 14224

Written by: E.C. Andrews
Edited by: Elise Carraway
Designed by: Amelia Harris

Cataloging-in-Publication Data
Names: Andrews, E.C.
Title: When your family moves / E.C. Andrews.
Description: Buffalo, NY : Kidhaven Publishing, 2026. | Series: A Guide to Change | Includes glossary and index
Identifiers: ISBN 9781534550155 (pbk) | ISBN 9781534550162 (library bound) | ISBN 9781534550179 (ebook)
Subjects: LCSH: Change (Psychology)—Juvenile Literature | Moving (Households)—Juvenile Literature
Classification: LCC BF637.C4 A53 2026 | DDC 155.4--dc25

Manufactured in the United States of America

CPSIA compliance information: Batch #CSKH26
For further information contact Greenhaven Publishing LLC at 1-844-317-7404.

Please visit our website, www.greenhavenpublishing.com.
For a free color catalog of all our high-quality books, call toll free 1-844-317-7404 or fax 1-844-317-7405.

Find us on

Image Credits
All images are courtesy of Shutterstock.com, unless otherwise stated. Cover – Zakharchenko Anna, Ground Picture, Ewelina W. Recurring – Alenka Karabanova, RidiUmbrella. 4–5 – Jamarale, Ann in the uk, FamVeld, Halfpoint, Lithiumphoto. 6–7 – Max kegfire, Krakenimages.com, Q88, New Africa, Tenstudio. 8–9 – fizkes, Maryna_Auramchuk, mei yanotai. 10–11 – Krakenimages.com, fizkes, Fagreia. 12–13 – OlgaKhorkova, Kobee, fizkes, Alexxndr, feodarina, CuteDesigns. 14–15 – Prostock-studio, TEYRAMES, Sonya illustration. 16–17 – Arina P Habich, QiuQiu.art, Roman Samokhin, Bborriss.67, alinabuphoto, GoodStudio. 18–19 – Pixel-Shot, bokan. 20–21 – AS photo family, 220 Selfmade studio, Donkeyworx. 22–23 – Evgeny Atamanenko, Monkey Business Images.

Contents

WORDS THAT LOOK LIKE THIS CAN BE FOUND IN THE GLOSSARY ON PAGE 24.

Change Is All Around Us

The world around us is changing all the time. Daylight changes to darkness every day. Seasons change every few months. As people, we change throughout our lives. We get bigger as we grow up.

The people we know or the places we go may change as we grow up. Change can be exciting. However, you may find that some changes feel a bit scary at first.

WELCOMING A NEW BROTHER OR SISTER

STARTING A NEW SCHOOL

Moving Day

Moving means changing where you live. It can be a very big change. Whether you are moving down the street or across the country, moving could feel exciting, scary, or many other feelings.

YOU COULD EVEN FEEL EXCITED AND NERVOUS AT THE SAME TIME.

The time before moving might be very busy. You will probably have lots of packing to do. Packing means putting all of your things in boxes to take with you.

GROWN-UPS MAY ALSO BE BUSY WITH LOTS OF PAPERWORK.

Why Do I Feel This Way?

Having big feelings because of change is normal. It is OK to feel worried or scared. You may be unsure about what might happen. Many people feel nervous when they are unsure.

EVEN GROWN-UPS CAN FEEL WORRIED WHEN BIG CHANGES HAPPEN.

It is OK if you feel happy or excited. You may be looking forward to seeing new places and doing new things. It is OK if you are feeling all these things.

THERE IS NO WRONG WAY TO FEEL WHEN BIG CHANGES HAPPEN.

Think About Your Feelings

When you have lots of big feelings, it can be hard to understand them. Taking big, deep breaths can help you notice and understand your feelings.

As you breathe, think about what you are feeling and why. It is OK if you do not know the answers.

YOU COULD TRY NAMING YOUR FEELINGS.

Talk About Your Feelings

Talking about your feelings can help you feel more understood. Talk to a trusted grown-up. Practicing what you want to say might help you before you say what you are feeling out loud.

IF YOU ARE NOT SURE WHAT TO SAY, TRY WRITING YOUR FEELINGS DOWN.

When you talk to a grown-up, find somewhere you feel comfortable. Try breaking your feelings up into simple sentences.

I feel ___ because ___ .

When I think about ___, I feel ___ .

I am not sure why, but I feel ___ .

Coping with Change

There are things that can help you feel more ready for change. Ask questions about your new house. Knowing what to expect may help you feel more confident.

WHAT IS IT LIKE?

HOW MANY ROOMS DOES IT HAVE?

WHERE IS IT?

YOU MIGHT BE ABLE TO VISIT YOUR NEW HOUSE BEFORE YOU MOVE.

Keeping some things the same can also help you cope with big changes. Doing the same things each day is called having a routine. Sticking to your usual routine can help your new house feel more familiar.

YOUR ROUTINE COULD INCLUDE THE TIME YOU GET UP OR GO TO BED.

Make Your Memories

A memory box is somewhere you can keep your special memories of where you used to live. You can look through your box when you want to remember those times. Here's how you make one!

- First, choose a box.
- Fill it with photographs, letters, and other things that make you happy.
- Decorate your box.

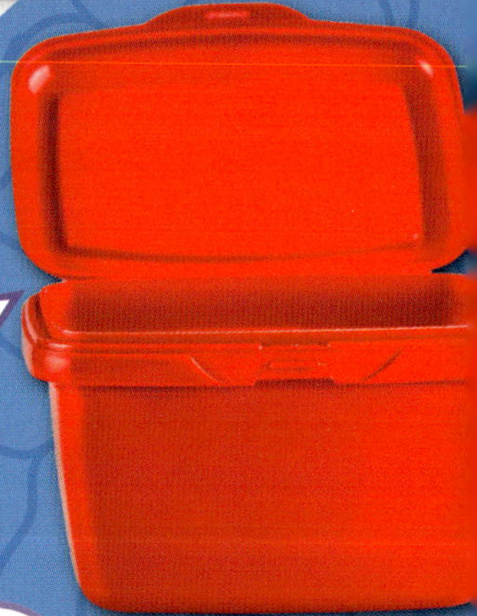

If you prefer, you could make a memory book.

- Choose a notebook.
- Stick happy memories in it, such as photographs, letters, or drawings.
- You could draw your own pictures on the pages or use it to write things down.
- Decorate the cover.

Decorate Your Space

When you move, you will get a new bedroom. This can be exciting. However, it is OK if you also feel worried. You may feel that you will miss your old room.

Choose a wall in your room. Decorate it with your favorite posters, pictures, letters, or photographs. You could even use things from your memory book or box. This will help your new room feel familiar.

ALWAYS ASK A GROWN-UP BEFORE DRAWING OR PAINTING ON THE WALLS.

Fun Times with Friends

Whether you are moving far away or down the road, keeping in touch with your friends could help this change feel less scary. Try inviting your friends over to see your new house.

THIS CAN MAKE EXPLORING YOUR NEW HOUSE EVEN MORE EXCITING!

If you are moving far away, try talking to your friends on the phone. If you can, try having your friends on a video call and giving them a tour of your new house.

Embracing Change

Big changes can cause big feelings. You may feel good. You may also feel nervous, worried, sad, or angry. These feelings are normal and OK to have.

IT IS OK TO FEEL A MIXTURE OF EMOTIONS.

Change can be fun and exciting. Try using some of the tips and tricks from this book to help you work through your big feelings. Soon, your new house will feel like home!

Glossary

anxious	**worried, scared, or uneasy**
familiar	**already known to you and recognizable**
trusted	**believed to be truthful, honest, and reliable**

Index